Dreams About Benjamin Franklin

Roshan B. Karki

ISBN: 9798371536501

DEDICATION

To everyone who knows me as Roshan B. Karki!

CONTENTS

ACKNOWLEDGMENTS

POEMS ABOUT BENJAMIN FRANKLIN AND OTHER U.S PRESIDENTS

A Five Hundred Dollar Bill

If I could mint coins and make money
There are great presidents already
On beautiful dollar bills.
If I had a chance to
make a five hundred dollar note
I will put portraits
of President Barack Obama in it.

You may ask why?
His presidency were times of joy
And were a golden period in history.
Benjamin Franklin is on hundred dollar note
And President Obama should be on
Five hundred dollar note.
Cause I saw legacy and history
in his days of Presidency.

A Painting of a U.S President

If I could paint well
with twelve different colors
and three cardinal colors
on a canvass
slowly and swiftly
like any U.S president's presidency
painting the eyes and hairs
I would paint Benjamin Franklin

You may ask why?
Because he was a genius and kind
And made the world
And made America
What it is today
And mostly he is in our hearts.

Dreams from Benjamin Franklin

I saw the founding father of United States.
He was wearing a thick spectacles in my dream.
He came to me and said, "Son! I will guide you.
You can be a legend."

I was a small boy back then
who wanted to be someone like Benjamin Franklin.
I did not know how
but the dream hanged like
a moon in my life.

I searched many pavements.
I searched many hearts.
I became a writer,
selling books in a cart.

And somehow the destiny followed
as I walked on the roads.
A dream, a desire and hard work is all there is
to be a legend.

I still see Benjamin Franklin in my dreams.

Existence of Benjamin Franklin

You are in a hundred dollar note
and I have a bill in pocket.
And in the cold winter nights
I will drink wine with it.

You are in my heart
as a founding father.
And In the summer nights
I will weave dream with it.

You are in history
and I read your books and legacy.
My only desire is
to be like you President Franklin.

If you make my Statue

I am not the President Right now.
But wants to be a one someday.
If you made my statue
remembering my poems and prose,
as my writings are worth
Make it near Barack Obama's statue.

He has made me heart warm
and to people and worlds.
And I plan to lay
my life and legacy behind.
If by any chance you make my statue,
make one near Barack Obama's Statue.

Like Benjamin Franklin

Late at nights
I look at mirror
And I am happy
My face has small wrinkles
And it makes me warm
As I have started
Looking like Benjamin Franklin.

On the mid days
I am thinking and writing speeches.
And I am happy
I am someone.
And it makes my heart warm
I am doing something
like Benjamin Franklin.

One hundred Benjamin Franklins

We will solve all problems of the world
from ozone layer depletion to climate change.
We will stay as brothers.
I wonder what the world will be
If there are one hundred Benjamin Franklins.

We will come up with new inventions.
We will solve poverty and stop terrorism.
Let there be more legends.
I wonder what the world will be like
If there are one hundred Benjamin Franklins.

Portraits of U.S Presidents

A dollar bill has George Washington.
A twenty dollar bills has Thomas Jefferson.
A fifty dollar bill has Abram Lincoln.
A hundred dollar note has Benjamin Franklin.
No wonder why money is so powerful.

And the U.S presidents
Worked for humanity
And brightened the world.
And I want to be in dollar bills
Like Benjamin Franklin.
No wonder why money is so powerful.

President of my Reality

I dream of being a president
and the dream came true.
But I am not in white house.
I am in a hut
as a president of my life.
I had my days of sorrow.
I had my days of joy.
Now the world sees as a hero.
I am president of my reality.
The good days are about to roll.

The Best People Ever

The white house is a home
to mostly talented minds
and mostly great leaders.
And each four or eight years
It's home to another mind
who will leave a legacy behind
In people's heart and places.
The world belongs to you
The brightest minds ever.
And great noble leaders
White House is a home
For centuries long
To best people ever.

POEMS ABOUT SOCIETY, OBJECTS AND PEOPLE

A Man at Work

Hurrying the man wakes up in the morning.
He then looks at the sun and plans the day.
He was very young when he started working.
And he has sustained his family with it every day.

He is a carpenter. He craves poetry in his woods.
His work has divinity and his hands has god in them.
Sometimes he hurries. Some time he slows.
The hours are swiftly turning like his hands the same.

Someday he will get old.
But his hands will still have divinity in them.
He has given a lot to the world
carving divinity with knives in woods.

May be we are music players, carpenters, poets or writers.
If you can do it well. Your hands will have god in them.

A Step Forward

Dare to move a step forward
Cause the humanity must do so
Sow the world with kindness and love
Victory lies somewhere in the path.

Dare to move a step forward
We are passengers on a journey
Let's follow legends and heroes
The world will be better doing so.

Let's take a step forward !

As the Generation Grows

As the generation grows,
they are getting soft and tender.
They have high visions and
to their visions the world surrenders.

As the generation grows
they are getting more spiritual.
It's a brave new world
but their heart is like flower.

They want to dance, party and sing.
And understand the enigma of being a human being.
They will solve the problems of the worlds.
And make people warm who are shivering in cold.

The generation is getting braver.
The generation is getting clever.
The generation is getting stronger.
The generation is getting more spiritual.

As the Passion Burns

It taunts me,
me and my passion
and burns like gasoline
as I write poetry

It makes my heart warm,
me and my passion
and warms me like a bonfire
as I write poetry

Beautiful American Girls

Some girls are exotic.
The American girls are wonderful.
Nancy Sinatra and Marilyn Monroe
are the proofs.
They are tempting my heart away.
American girls are beautiful.

The drink finest wine and drink coffee.
They have their favorite stars and toffees.
Their hair has multiple colors.
American girls! Do not make me go to troubles.

They shake your body in Discotheque
as if they are immortals,
from white to fair are their colors.
American girls are beautiful as flowers.

And it's been five minutes
Since I kisses your lips
And bought you drink.
An hour ago you were total stranger.

American girls are very beautiful.

Eve of Battle

It's eve of battle
and the horses are ready.
The moon is watching us.
We are studying our enemies.

The iron armor is cold.
It will get warm with sun shine tomorrow.
The history of tomorrow's battle will be told
to our children and to their children.

So raise the sails.
What is there to worry?
Tomorrow we will head for victory.
It's the eve of battle.

Soldiers! Be ready

Fighting for Humanity

I stay up late at night making speeches
and I think for humanity.
I won't let the wind stop me.
We are better. The best is yet to be.

The world need more leaders
And being a leader is not very easy.
You got to make the world follow you
and your speeches should heal humanity.

And when you do so,
the whole generation will follow.
You will appear in TVs and magazine
and be written in pages of history.
Cause fighting for humanity is not very easy
but when you do so. It's worth it.

Flower in a Vase

I watched a seed grow into flower
in a vase made of glass.
And the seed grew every hour
As if the vase was its nest.

And when the shrub bloomed
it looked youthful.
The branches were its body.
The flower was its breasts.
The moon shines above with a crest.

And it started looking for a lover
and it found it.
The flowers grew into fruits
and grew beautifully.

Please do not pluck the flowers.
Let them grow with youth, vigor
and find a lover.
Let them have fruits as children.

Gallery of History

An old man was at gallery of history.
He had his own tales. He had his own story.
Born in Iowa he had two daughters and a son.
His life childhood to now was mostly fun.

He married a girl from New York and moved there.
He had fun living with his family with love he shared.
He had his days of happiness. He has days of tears
He had his own hobbies which never withered.

He gifted his wife with presents he could afford.
He drove a modest car made by Ford.
He watched the snowflakes and tides in a sea.
He harvested crops and honey from honey bee.

The old man is all gone now.
He has reached history somehow.
I read his tales drinking tea.
Working class hero is something to be.

Gloomy Moon

Away from the world
The gloomy moon lies
Like a moth in the skies
and shows sadness when
People make love in their homes .

The sky is all alone
That's explains why
The lord placed
A moth in the skies.
But the stars are clear at night.
The gloomy moon lies
among the clouds.

Somebody find a partner
And make the moon happy
Let the gloomy moon shine.

Lady with the Lamp II

Lady with the lamp
Carries her lantern
In cold and damp
Yet, a nurse she has
Smile on her face
She had kindness in her heart.
Which everyone can trace.

The patients has glow on her face
in her presence.
The soldiers are wounded.
The battle field is tense.
She wishes the battle would end
as she hears soldiers crying in pain.

She has healed thousands
and will heal thousands more.
And even in the midnights
she is working.
She is a human, nurse
and a messenger of peace.
She is also a savior.

Listening to Led Zeppelin

It is said that history repeats itself
But the history made by Led Zeppelin
Is not repeated yet.
The songs are pure magic
and I travel to galaxies and seas
as I listen Led Zeppelin.

I feel I am travelling
On the stairway to heaven
With my black dog
Giving all of my love to you.
And I ramble on
As I sing Immigrant song
To gods in Kashmir.
Sometimes I feel
I am going to California
On a road trip
with Robert plant and Jimmy Page
As I listen Led Zeppelin.

Lover of Life

I am lover of life
More than a rebel
My soul hangs in the sky
As I lie in bed.

My soul travels
across stars, moon and constellations.
I drink wine and play music
and dress myself in latest fashion.

I treat everyone equally.
I love my life heart fully.
I had my days of revolution.
I have understood the world and people.

Now I am a lover of life.

Middle Class Family

Under the roof
We have world of our own
We gaze the stars at night
We wake up with sun.

Each Friday we drink wine.
You are mine. I'm yours.
Each Sunday we go to mass.
Rest of the day we hurry to schools and jobs.

New movies, songs keep us entertained.
my son plays guitar. My daughter paints.
Our jobs has kept the family sustained.
We are a middle class family.
We are heroes in our own world.

Nobody's Home

It's been years the house is left,
the couples left the village in search
Of future and shimmering cities.
Probably they moved to Paris and New York.
Careful passengers! Nobody's home.

Someday they will return
when they are old and tired.
They will leave their children in shimmering cities.
They have searched for future.
Now they will seek past.
But today the house is all alone.
Careful passengers! Nobody's home.

Schools

We will build dreams
Brick by brick
Like our school is
And be a man someday.

My mother asks,
"Do you have a girlfriend?"
I say no.
Doing so will make me in troubles.
But I secretly like Leah.

I work hard
to bring marks.
And my favorite movie
is forest Gump.

At night I listen to Beethoven
and practice math.
I have to work hard
to walk in a town
as a man someday.

Some Dreams come true

Some dreams come true
The dreams you dreamed
When you were alone.
And when the dream comes true
People come to you.

Some dreams come true.
The dreams that were dreamed
When your pockets were empty
And you were hungry.
And when the dream come true.
People cherish for you.

Sun in the winter

Rest of the world is covered with snow.
And the sun is unhappy being so.
He can melt the glaciers but not snowflakes
falling slowly as snow.

The white wilderness in beautiful.
It's time for New Year and Christmas.
But the lovers like to stay in sun
and melt their hearts like snow.

The Birds

Up high in the sky
the birds call for freedom
are they too chained to the sky?

Up night in the sky
the birds fly
Do they know where heaven lies?

My heart aches
as I want fly in the sky.

The Violin Player

There is a violin player
playing in the streets of California
Composing prophetic themes.

She is no rich
but her compositions are.
And one night she got a chance
to play violin in a fancy bar.

She sang about seven layers of heaven.
She sang about dreams.
And a record company found her.

If you understand her music.
Her violin tells about
Events, future and prophecies.

Now she has home and a car
she plays violin in cozy bars.
People cheer for her.

Her music composed in the streets
are now solid hits.

And I feel heaven
when I am listen to the violin.
For I am the violin player
who started composing from the streets.

Wine will Change few things

May be its church or a bar
We still have miles to go
We have come this far
We might have to walk in snow
Wine will change few things.

Cheers! Go take a sip of divinity
You will feel warm
You will feel beauty
You will feel vigor like tides in a sea
Wine will change few things.

So empty your glasses.
What is there to worry?
Since the last drink
I am five minutes old already
Wine will change few things.

Wine will Change few things

May be its church or a bar
We still have miles to go
We have come this far
We might have to walk in snow
Wine will change few things.

Cheers! Go take a sip of divinity
You will feel warm
You will feel beauty
You will feel vigor like tides in a sea
Wine will change few things.

So empty your glasses.
What is there to worry?
Since the last drink
I am five minutes old already
Wine will change few things.

Wine will Change few things

May be its church or a bar
We still have miles to go
We have come this far
We might have to walk in snow
Wine will change few things.

Cheers! Go take a sip of divinity
You will feel warm
You will feel beauty
You will feel vigor like tides in a sea
Wine will change few things.

So empty your glasses.
What is there to worry?
Since the last drink
I am five minutes old already
Wine will change few things.

POEMS ABOUT MYTHICAL SUBJECTS

Enigma and the World

The great pyramids are standing
As wonder and enigma
And I will keep on writing
creating miracles and beauty with the words.

Jesus could do miracles
and walk on the water.
For I too feel I am a prophet with pens.
And my words fly in the space like shooting stars.

There are poverty to be solved,
wars to be conducted and wars to be stopped.
Help me rule the world someday
creating legacy and actions with the world.

My pen
My ink
My words
My verse
Stands between enigma and the world.

In search of Mermaids

The sky was dark.
The moon was on sky.
The dog's in the streets bark.
And I decided to leave my home
in search for mermaids.

The peasants worked on fields,
fueling upon the farm's yield.
They farm and they haunted.
But nobody till now left home
in search for mermaids.

So I sailed on a river.
The River took me to sea.
I met thousands of passengers
but no one knew
where the mermaids existed.

I decided to return back
Then I found you on human form
Like Jesus was to God's.
We are living myths and histories.
God must have changed you to

a mermaid and girl from Eve
in the forbidden garden,
Where we all lay.

Lost City of Atlantis

The lost city of Atlantis whispers an old man's name.
The whispers says, "Before I was a king now I am a lame."
The city is under sea bed with its sacred geometry.
Now, nymphs and mermaids are its infantry.
Lost and unknown to the world sacred knowledge lies there.
Let the ancient sacred knowledge come. Let's not fear.
Cause I am a mystic in search of ancient knowledge and treasures.
And the lost king whispers to me in a voice so clear.
Each day voice comes to me and I am near
with its lost ancient knowledge buries under seas.
The city was under sea bed with enigma and trees.
Some say an apple tree lied there where there was a snake.
And couples like Adam and Eve joined the snake with hand shake.
But the story is different than that of Garden of Eden.
The lost city is full of sacred knowledge and with gold boxes it's laden.
Let me bring the treasures and secrets to this world.
And I will take the world to the path not yet told.

Out of Body Experiences to San Francisco

I rested on a bed
and my soul flew across space.
It flied like a feather
and reached San Francisco.

I watched the golden gate bridge from a height.
The people looked beautiful from skies.
I looked down at the Yosemite Park.
And watched the dolphins and Sharks.

My soul flew like a dove
and people in San Francisco were so much in love.
I feel nirvana and peace
as my soul flew to San Francisco.

POEMS ABOUT LOVE

As Wide as the Seas

I love you
as wide as the seas
as narrow as a ray of light.

Raise the sails
as we search for treasures
under Sea bed

The waves are unanswered
so is our love

The sea will never grow old
so we will

It's midnight
the tides will be high.
Hold me in your arms tonight.

Last Poem for Tonight

You are not home
and I am dabbling my mind with poetry.
I am all alone
and you light up the pages with your beauty.

When you come home
I will read it to you aloud.
And I will be with you tonight
looking at the stars and the clouds.

We will gather in balcony.
The world is lover's colony.
And I will read it aloud to you,
the last poem for tonight.

Love as you are

The seas
and tides jump
as they are

The stars
And the moon shine
as they are

Fall in love
with yourself and the people
as you are.

Something Better

I found something better to do
since the day I met you.
We shook our hands
and there are memories which time cannot undo.

Your reflection comes in my mind
and blows in my heart away
like a desert in the wind .
And it was time to start something new.

I shared lips with you
and wanted to be a better version.
I started doing something new
and that's reflect paper on you as poetry.

The Lost Train Tracks

I stood by the train tracks
the iron bars were rusted.
And we joined our hearts
When we first met
You were waiting for trains
Carrying a purse
You had a flower in your hair
And your beauty drew me near
Like a soldier
Drawing his sword slowly
And you wounded me
With your love
And the next day
You healed me
And my teardrops fall
On the lost train tracks.

BONUS SHORT POEMS ABD HAIKUS

A Soldier

Fighting for justice
He will throw his life away
with swords

My Best Friend

Flesh and blood
we are bound
with childhood and love

On Your Shadows

You sat by the trees shadow
and I sat by your shadow
Calmness for the both

The Dragon and the Mermaid

The dragon breathes fire
the mermaid dances it with
under the sea bed

The Moon and the Cocoon

Somebody sleeps in cocoon
it dreams of being a butterfly
but flies to world as a moth

ABOUT THE AUTHOR

Roshan B. Karki (Roshan Bikram Kark) is a poet, writer, musician, entrepreneur and politician. He was born in Kathmandu, Nepal. He has attended Loras College, USA as an honors student to pursue undergraduate in Creative writing. "Dreams from Benjamin Franklin" is twenty second book by the author. He publishes his book independently via create space. Although he is an Asian his creative sources include western writers and western philosophy. His books have appeared worldwide on major online websites. His major genres are poetry, science fiction, political science and fantasy. In the coming days with the help from readers he aims to publish his books physically and go on world tours reading poetry. Please give his books a read and welcome the new genre of writing!

www.ingramcontent.com/pod-product-compliance
Lightning Source LLC
LaVergne TN
LVHW050347160826
845677LV00014B/3831